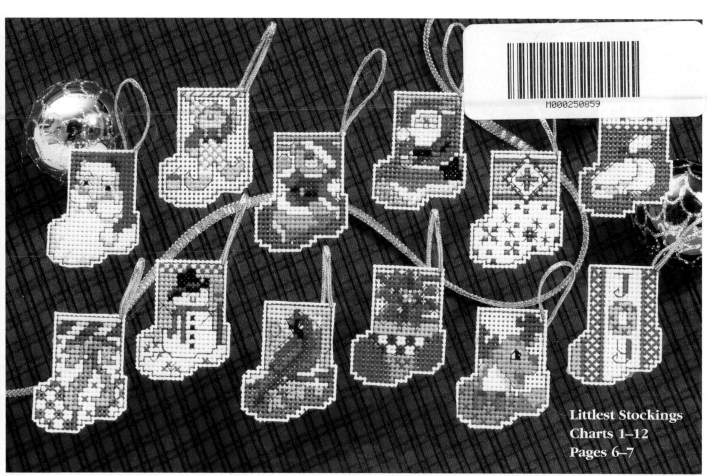

Littlest Stockings
Charts 1–12
Pages 6–7

Christmas Critters
Charts 13–24
Pages 8–9

1

Winter Fun
Charts 25–30
Pages 10–11

Winter Fun
Charts 31–36
Pages 12–13

Let It Snow
Charts 47–51
Pages 19–21

Noah's Friends
Charts 57–60, 62
Pages 24–26

Let It Snow
Charts 52–56
Pages 21–23

Noah's Friends
Charts 61, 63–66
Pages 26–28

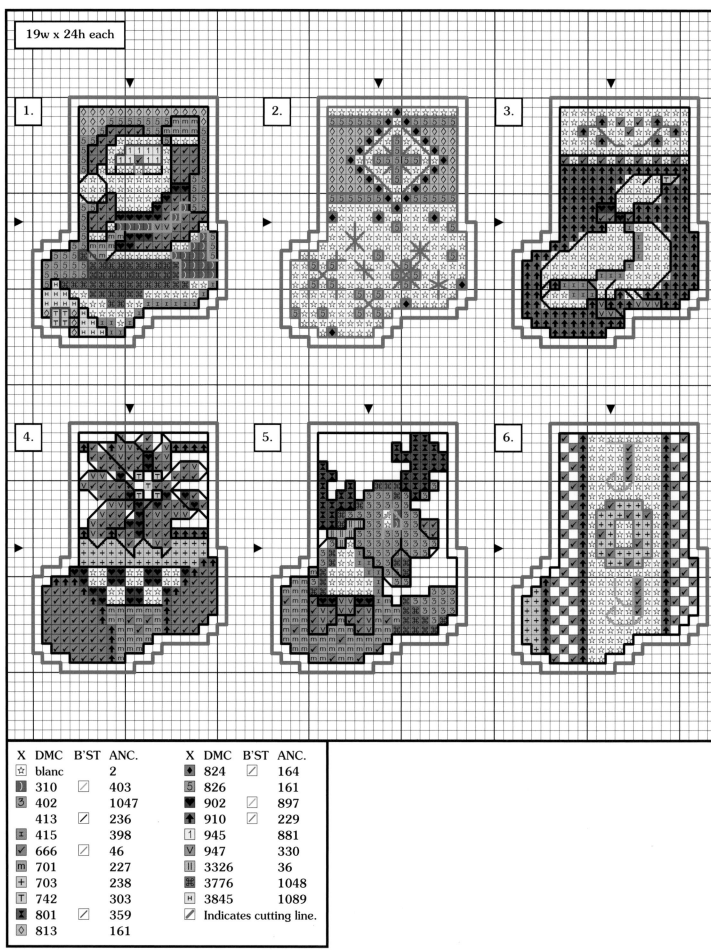

19w x 24h each

X	DMC	B'ST	ANC.		X	DMC	B'ST	ANC.
☆	blanc		2		◆	824	╱	164
◗	310	╱	403		5	826		161
3	402		1047		◆	902	╱	897
	413	╱	236		⬆	910	╱	229
I	415		398		1	945		881
✓	666	╱	46		V	947		330
m	701		227		‖	3326		36
+	703		238		⌘	3776		1048
T	742		303		H	3845		1089
✕	801	╱	359		╱	Indicates cutting line.		
◇	813		161					

Littlest Stockings Charts 1–6

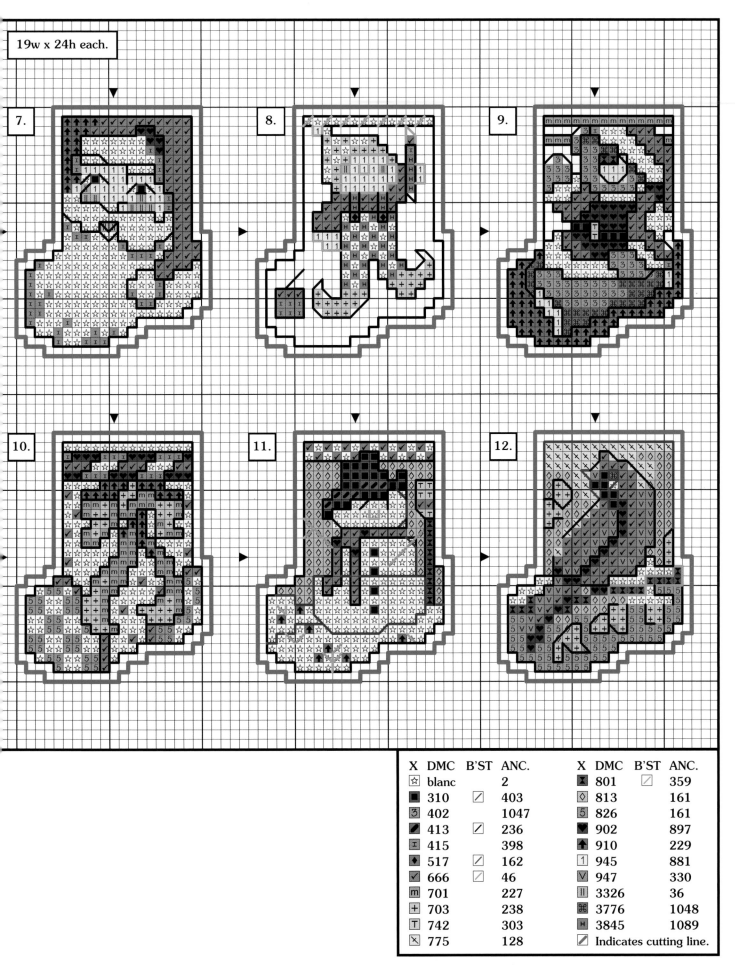

19w x 24h each.

X	DMC	B'ST	ANC.		X	DMC	B'ST	ANC.
☆	blanc		2		✕	801	◿	359
■	310	◿	403		◇	813		161
3	402		1047		5	826		161
◢	413	◿	236		♥	902		897
I	415		398		⬆	910		229
◆	517	◿	162		1	945		881
✔	666	◿	46		V	947		330
m	701		227		‖	3326		36
+	703		238		⌘	3776		1048
T	742		303		H	3845		1089
✕	775		128		◿	Indicates cutting line.		

Littlest Stockings Charts 7–12

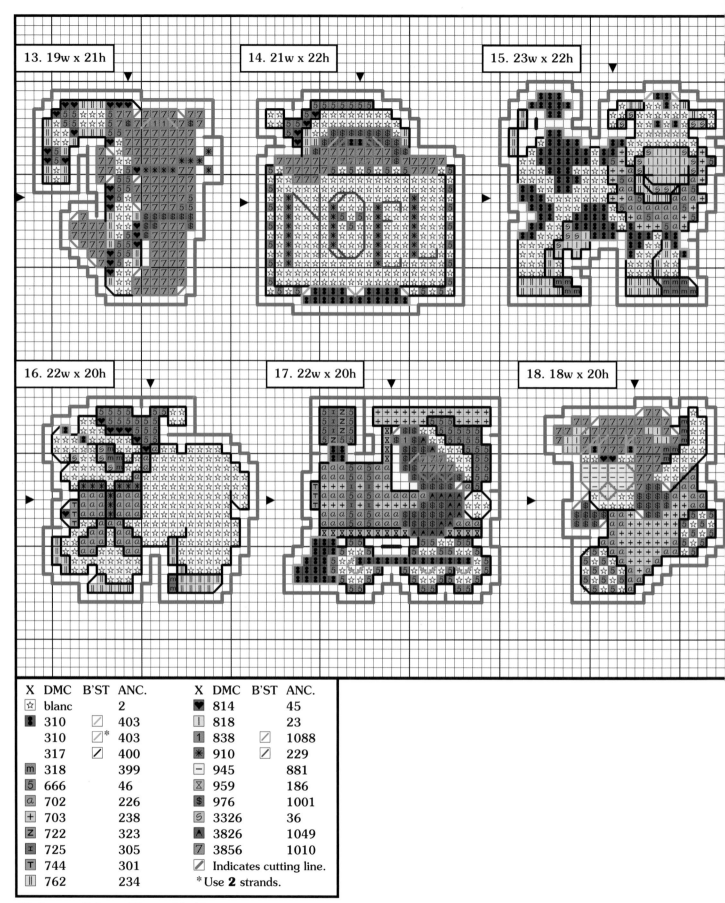

13. 19w x 21h

14. 21w x 22h

15. 23w x 22h

16. 22w x 20h

17. 22w x 20h

18. 18w x 20h

X	DMC	B'ST	ANC.	X	DMC	B'ST	ANC.
☆	blanc		2	♥	814		45
▮	310	◪	403	‖	818		23
	310	◪*	403	1	838	◪	1088
	317	◪	400	✳	910	◪	229
m	318		399	−	945		881
5	666		46	✕	959		186
a	702		226	$	976		1001
+	703		238	5	3326		36
z	722		323	▲	3826		1049
I	725		305	7	3856		1010
T	744		301	◪	Indicates cutting line.		
‖	762		234	*Use **2** strands.			

Christmas Critters Charts 13–18

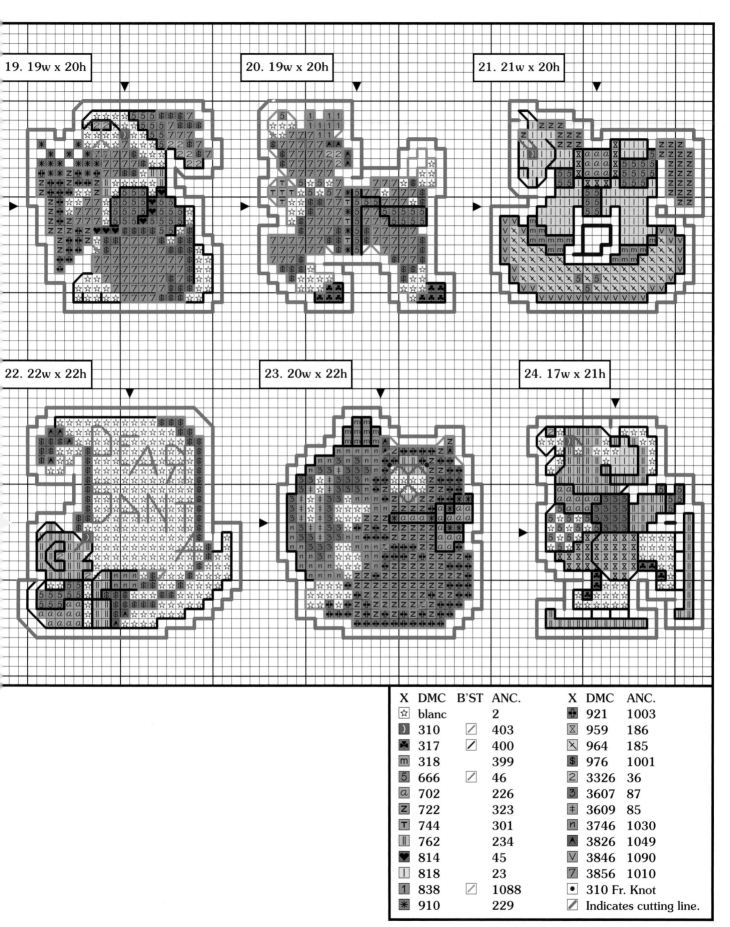

X	DMC	B'ST	ANC.		X	DMC	ANC.
☆	blanc		2		✚	921	1003
)	310	∕	403		⊠	959	186
✖	317	∕	400		⊠	964	185
m	318		399		$	976	1001
5	666	∕	46		2	3326	36
a	702		226		3	3607	87
z	722		323		‡	3609	85
T	744		301		n	3746	1030
‖	762		234		▲	3826	1049
♥	814		45		∨	3846	1090
I	818		23		7	3856	1010
1	838	∕	1088		•	310 Fr. Knot	
*	910		229		∕	Indicates cutting line.	

Christmas Critters Charts 19–24

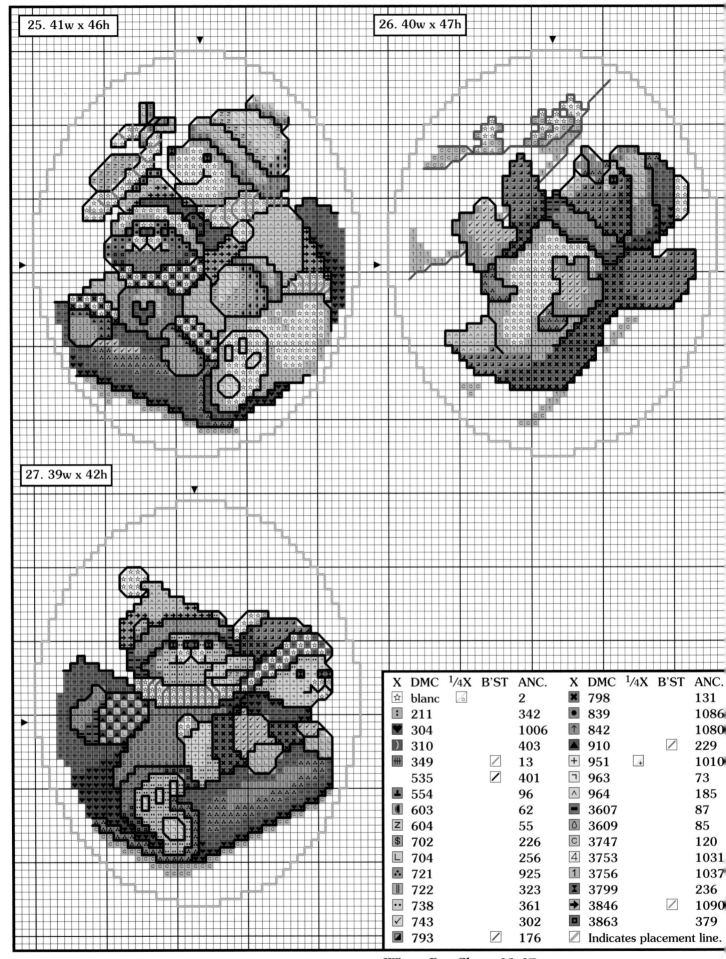

25. 41w x 46h

26. 40w x 47h

27. 39w x 42h

X	DMC	1/4X	B'ST	ANC.		X	DMC	1/4X	B'ST	ANC.
☆	blanc	☆		2		✖	798			131
:	211			342		●	839			1086
♥	304			1006		↑	842			1080
)	310			403		▲	910		◪	229
⊞	349		◪	13		+	951	+		1010
	535		◪	401		⌐	963			73
⬛	554			96		^	964			185
◖	603			62		▬	3607			87
z	604			55		◊	3609			85
$	702			226		C	3747			120
L	704			256		4	3753			1031
∴	721			925		1	3756			1037
‖	722			323		✕	3799			236
∵	738			361		➜	3846		◪	1090
✓	743			302		◨	3863			379
◪	793		◪	176		◪	Indicates placement line.			

Winter Fun Charts 25–27

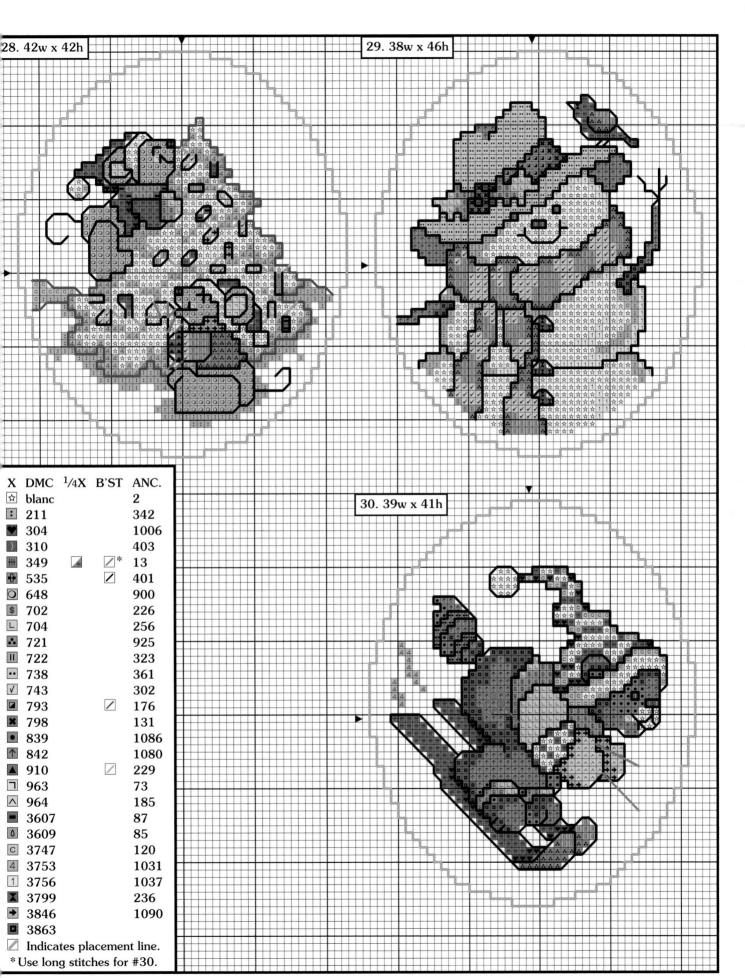

X	DMC	¼X	B'ST	ANC.
☆	blanc			2
⠿	211			342
♥	304			1006
◖	310			403
⊞	349	◢	╱*	13
⊞	535		╱	401
◯	648			900
$	702			226
⌐	704			256
❖	721			925
‖	722			323
••	738			361
√	743			302
◩	793		╱	176
✖	798			131
●	839			1086
↑	842			1080
▲	910		╱	229
⌐	963			73
∧	964			185
■	3607			87
◊	3609			85
⒞	3747			120
④	3753			1031
①	3756			1037
✖	3799			236
➡	3846			1090
◲	3863			

╱ Indicates placement line.
* Use long stitches for #30.

Winter Fun Charts 28–30

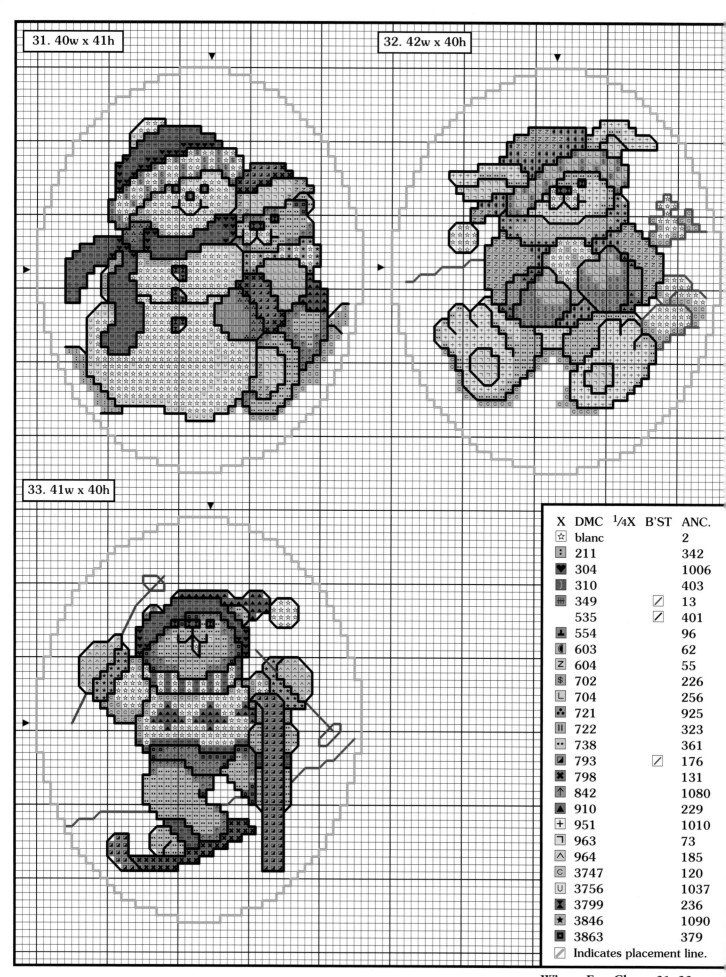

31. 40w x 41h

32. 42w x 40h

33. 41w x 40h

X	DMC	¼X	B'ST	ANC.
☆	blanc			2
⋮	211			342
♥	304			1006
◐	310			403
▦	349		╱	13
	535		╱	401
⊥	554			96
◖	603			62
Z	604			55
$	702			226
L	704			256
⋰	721			925
‖	722			323
⋯	738			361
◪	793		╱	176
✖	798			131
↑	842			1080
▲	910			229
+	951			1010
⌐	963			73
∧	964			185
C	3747			120
U	3756			1037
✕	3799			236
★	3846			1090
◩	3863			379
╱	Indicates placement line.			

Winter Fun Charts 31–33

12

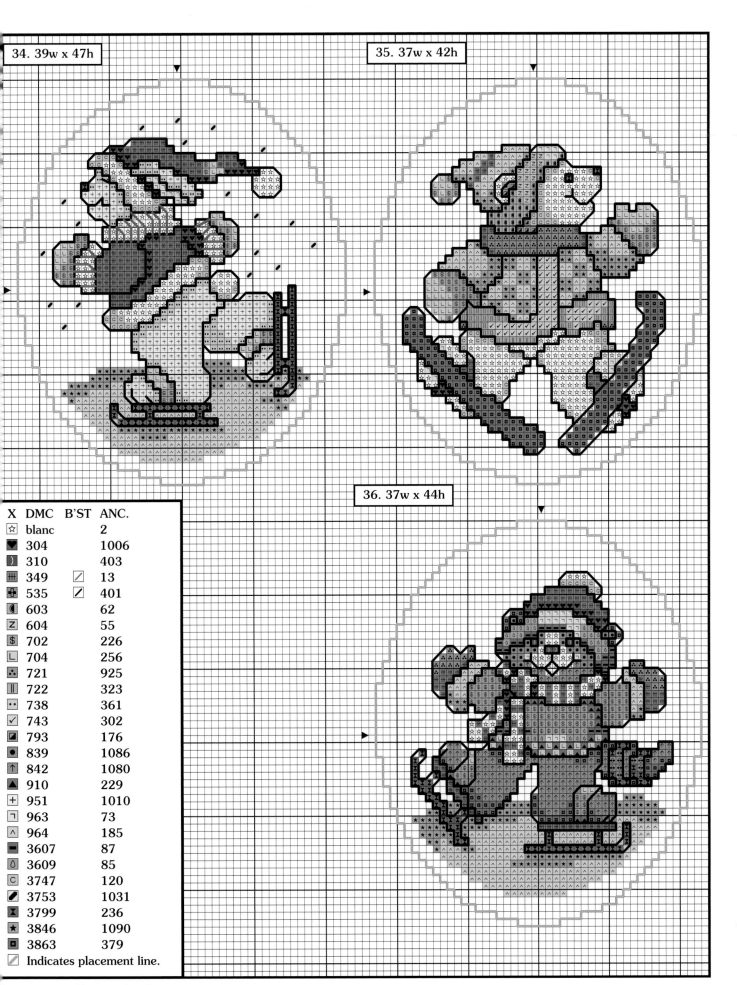

34. 39w x 47h

35. 37w x 42h

36. 37w x 44h

X	DMC	B'ST	ANC.
☆	blanc		2
♥	304		1006
◖	310		403
⊞	349	⟋	13
✚	535	⟋	401
◖	603		62
Z	604		55
$	702		226
L	704		256
∴	721		925
‖	722		323
∷	738		361
✓	743		302
◪	793		176
●	839		1086
↑	842		1080
▲	910		229
+	951		1010
⌐	963		73
^	964		185
▬	3607		87
◊	3609		85
C	3747		120
◣	3753		1031
✕	3799		236
★	3846		1090
▣	3863		379
⟋	Indicates placement line.		

Winter Fun Charts 34–36

13

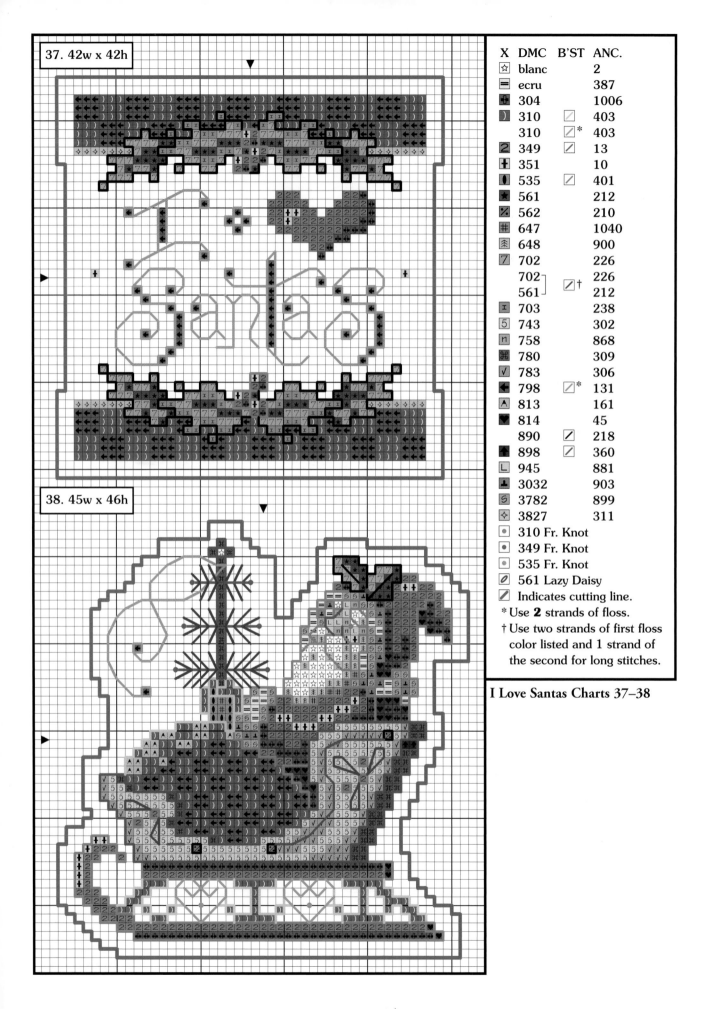

37. 42w x 42h

38. 45w x 46h

X	DMC	B'ST	ANC.
☆	blanc		2
=	ecru		387
✠	304		1006
◗	310	◿	403
	310	◿*	403
2	349	◿	13
✚	351		10
▮	535	◿	401
★	561		212
◹	562		210
▦	647		1040
▩	648		900
7	702		226
	702 ⎤	◿†	226
	561 ⎦		212
I	703		238
5	743		302
n	758		868
▓	780		309
√	783		306
◀	798	◿*	131
▲	813		161
♥	814		45
	890	◿	218
◆	898	◿	360
L	945		881
▰	3032		903
6	3782		899
✧	3827		311
⊙	310 Fr. Knot		
•	349 Fr. Knot		
◦	535 Fr. Knot		
∅	561 Lazy Daisy		
◿	Indicates cutting line.		

* Use **2** strands of floss.

† Use two strands of first floss
color listed and 1 strand of
the second for long stitches.

I Love Santas Charts 37–38

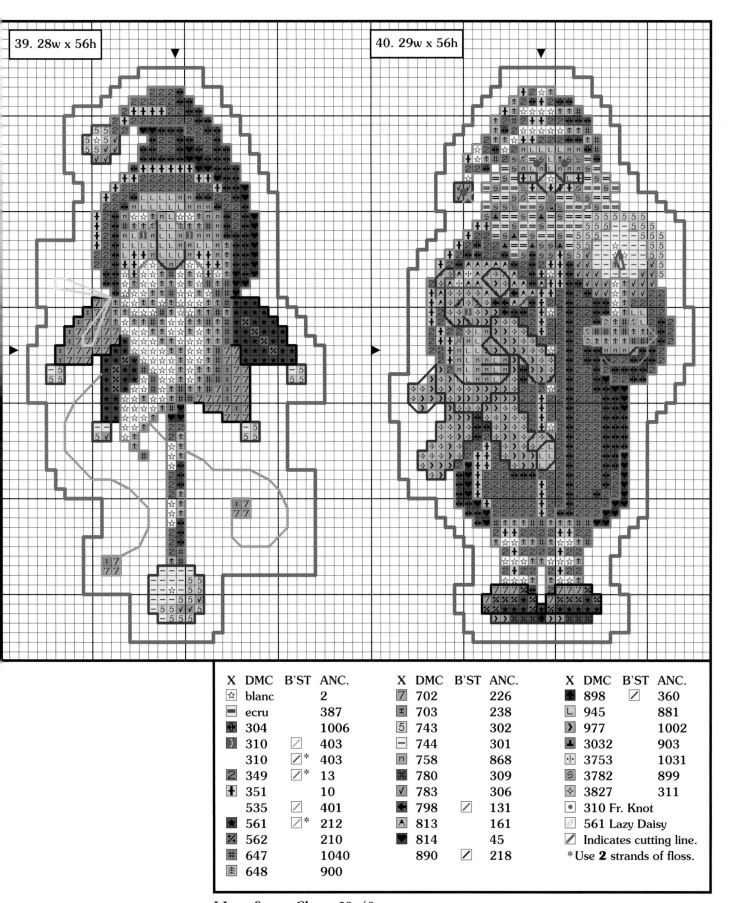

X	DMC	B'ST	ANC.	X	DMC	B'ST	ANC.	X	DMC	B'ST	ANC.
☆	blanc		2	7	702		226	✛	898	∕	360
=	ecru		387	I	703		238	L	945		881
✠	304		1006	5	743		302	〉	977		1002
◗	310	∕	403	−	744		301	⬥	3032		903
	310	∕*	403	n	758		868	⋅⊦⋅	3753		1031
2	349	∕*	13	⊞	780		309	5	3782		899
✛	351		10	✓	783		306	✧	3827		311
	535	∕	401	◀	798	∕	131	•	310 Fr. Knot		
★	561	∕*	212	⬥	813		161	∕	561 Lazy Daisy		
⊠	562		210	♥	814		45	∕	Indicates cutting line.		
⌗	647		1040		890	∕	218	*Use **2** strands of floss.			
✿	648		900								

I Love Santas Charts 39–40

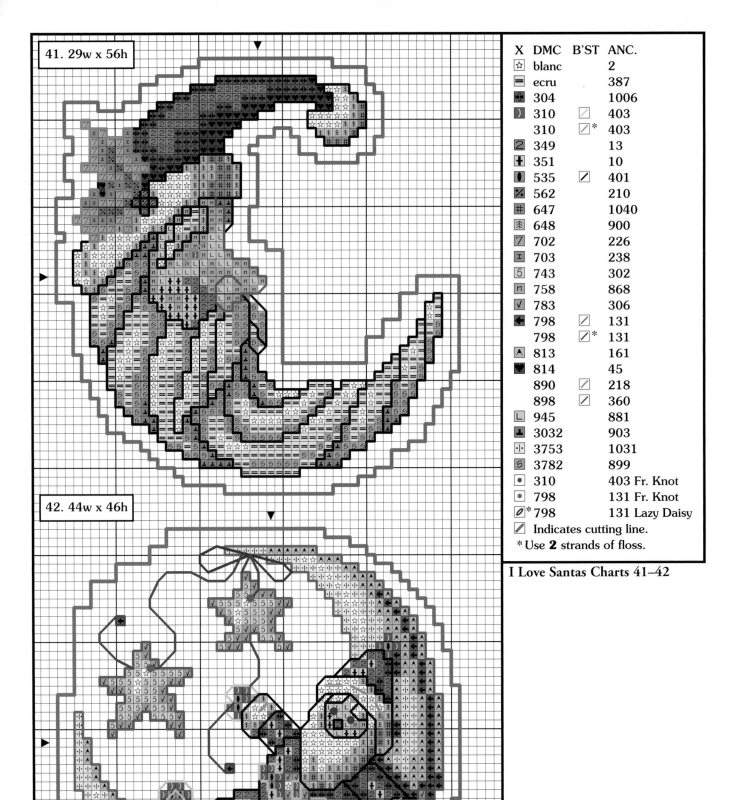

X	DMC	B'ST	ANC.
☆	blanc		2
=	ecru		387
✠	304		1006
)	310	╱	403
	310	╱*	403
2	349		13
✚	351		10
◖	535	╱	401
⁒	562		210
⊞	647		1040
⚘	648		900
7	702		226
I	703		238
5	743		302
n	758		868
√	783		306
◀	798	╱	131
	798	╱*	131
▲	813		161
♥	814		45
	890	╱	218
	898	╱	360
L	945		881
⊥	3032		903
⦙	3753		1031
5	3782		899
●	310		403 Fr. Knot
●	798		131 Fr. Knot
⊘*	798		131 Lazy Daisy
╱	Indicates cutting line.		
* Use **2** strands of floss.			

I Love Santas Charts 41–42

41. 29w x 56h

42. 44w x 46h

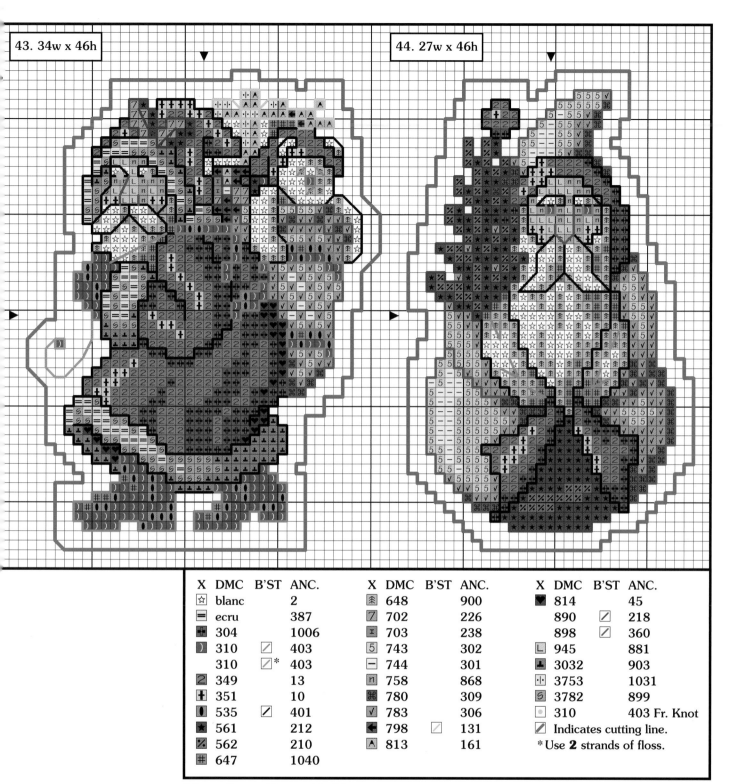

43. 34w x 46h

44. 27w x 46h

X	DMC	B'ST	ANC.	X	DMC	B'ST	ANC.	X	DMC	B'ST	ANC.
☆	blanc		2	�፠	648		900	♥	814		45
=	ecru		387	7	702		226		890	∕	218
✛	304		1006	⊥	703		238		898	∕	360
)	310	∕	403	5	743		302	L	945		881
	310	∕*	403	−	744		301	⊥	3032		903
2	349		13	n	758		868	·!·	3753		1031
✚	351		10	✹	780		309	S	3782		899
❘	535	∕	401	√	783		306	•	310		403 Fr. Knot
★	561		212	◀	798	∕	131	∕	Indicates cutting line.		
▨	562		210	◭	813		161	*Use **2** strands of floss.			
#	647		1040								

I Love Santas Charts 43–44

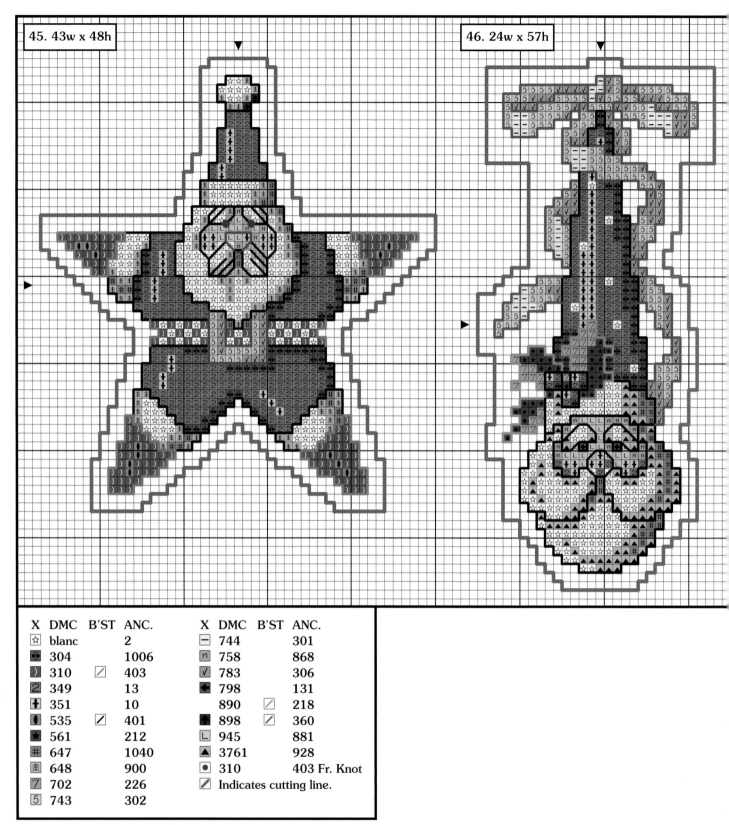

45. 43w x 48h

46. 24w x 57h

X	DMC	B'ST	ANC.	X	DMC	B'ST	ANC.
☆	blanc		2	−	744		301
✚	304		1006	n	758		868
◗	310	╱	403	√	783		306
2	349		13	◄	798		131
✚	351		10		890	╱	218
◖	535	╱	401	◼	898	╱	360
★	561		212	L	945		881
⊞	647		1040	▲	3761		928
✸	648		900	●	310		403 Fr. Knot
7	702		226	╱	Indicates cutting line.		
5	743		302				

I Love Santas Charts 45–46

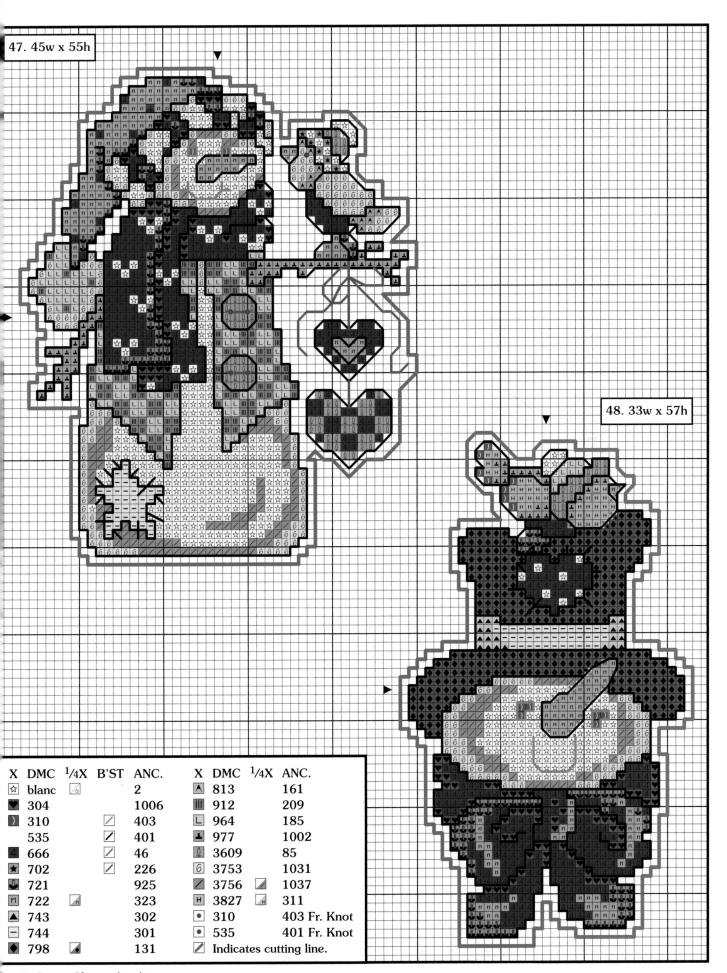

47. 45w x 55h

48. 33w x 57h

X	DMC	1/4X	B'ST	ANC.		X	DMC	1/4X	ANC.
☆	blanc	◪		2		▲	813		161
♥	304			1006		▥	912		209
⟩	310		╱	403		∟	964		185
	535		╱	401		♨	977		1002
◩	666		╱	46		⚲	3609		85
★	702		╱	226		6	3753		1031
↡	721			925		╱	3756	╱	1037
n	722	◪		323		H	3827	◪	311
▲	743			302		•	310		403 Fr. Knot
−	744			301		•	535		401 Fr. Knot
◆	798	◪		131		╱	Indicates cutting line.		

Let It Snow Charts 47–48

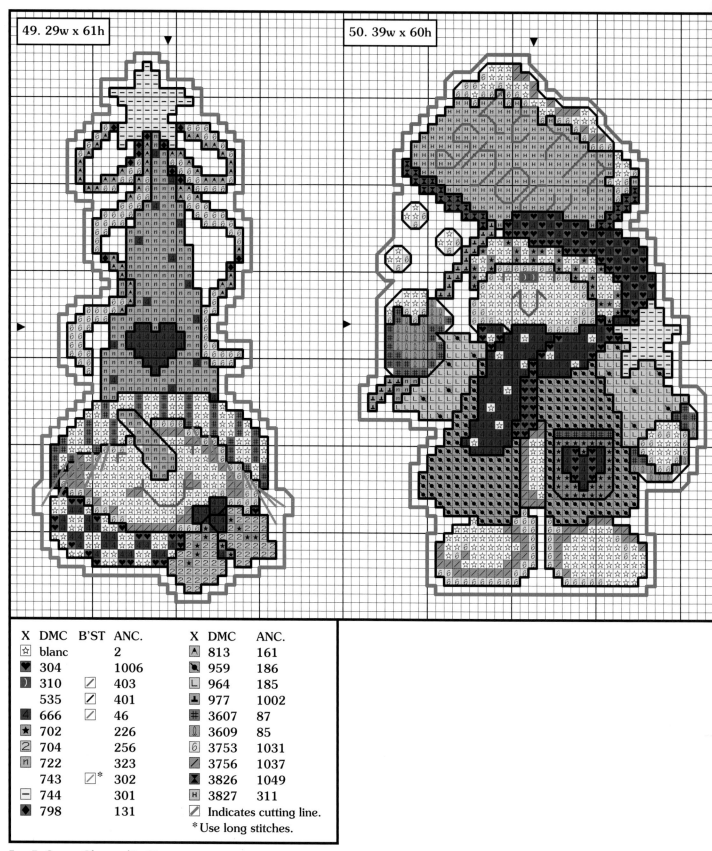

49. 29w x 61h   50. 39w x 60h

X	DMC	B'ST	ANC.		X	DMC	ANC.
☆	blanc		2		◣	813	161
♥	304		1006		◥	959	186
☽	310	∕	403		L	964	185
	535	∕	401		⊥	977	1002
◢	666	∕	46		#	3607	87
★	702		226		⓪	3609	85
2	704		256		6	3753	1031
n	722		323		∕	3756	1037
	743	∕ *	302		✕	3826	1049
−	744		301		H	3827	311
◆	798		131		∕	Indicates cutting line.	
						* Use long stitches.	

Let It Snow Charts 49–50

51. 40w x 60h

52. 44w x 55h

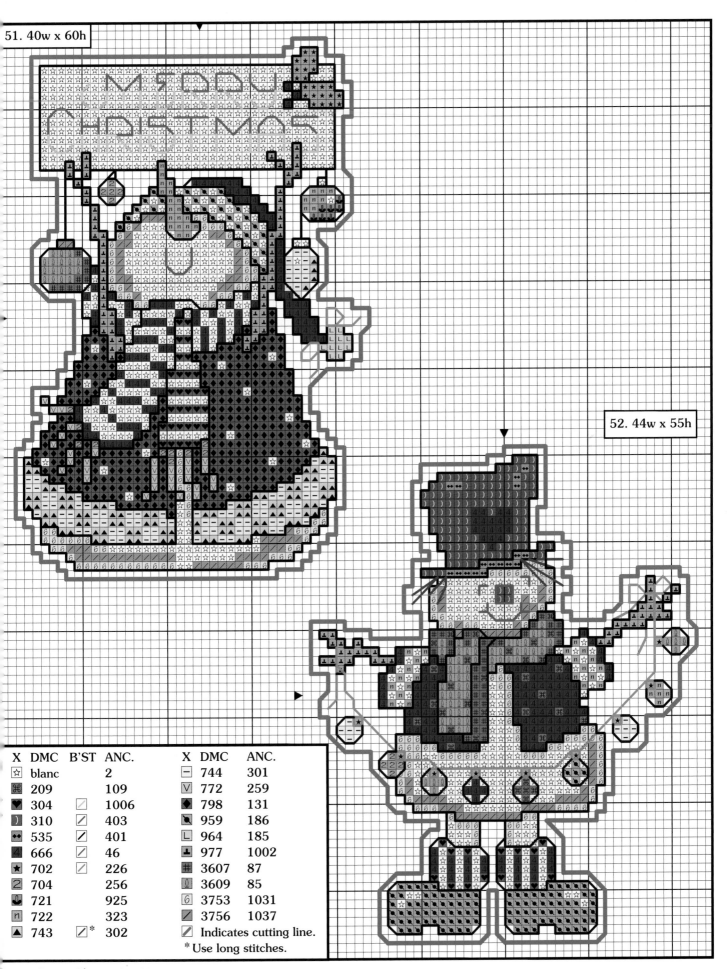

X	DMC	B'ST	ANC.		X	DMC	ANC.
☆	blanc		2		−	744	301
⌗	209		109		V	772	259
♥	304	∕	1006		◆	798	131
◖	310	∕	403		◣	959	186
◆◆	535	∕	401		L	964	185
4	666	∕	46		⊥	977	1002
★	702	∕	226		⌗	3607	87
2	704		256		0	3609	85
⛟	721		925		6	3753	1031
n	722		323		∕	3756	1037
▲	743	∕*	302		∕	Indicates cutting line.	

* Use long stitches.

Let It Snow Charts 51–52

53. 42w x 55h

54. 50w x 45h

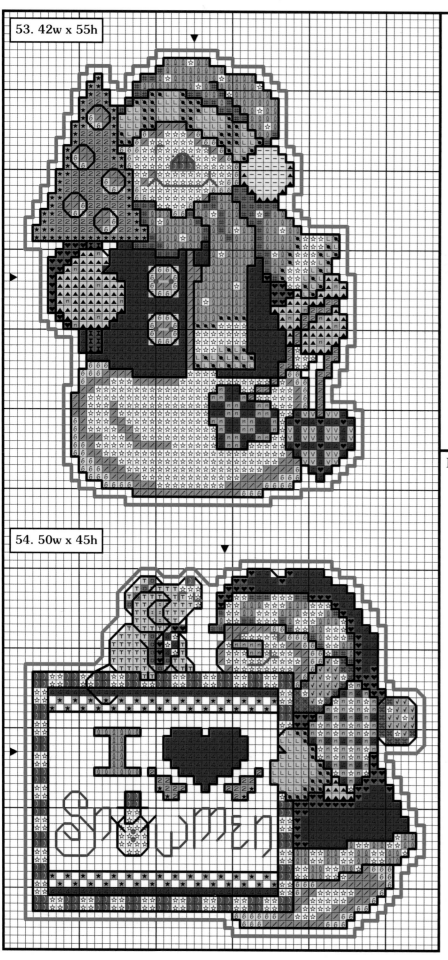

X	DMC	1/4X	B'ST	ANC.
☆	blanc	⊡		2
⌘	209		∕	109
√	211			342
♥	304			1006
☽	310	◣	∕	403
⊡	414			235
	535		∕	401
◢	666		∕	46
★	702			226
2	704			256
n	722			323
▲	743			302
−	744			301
V	772			259
◣	959			186
L	964			185
T	3072			847
I	3326			36
⊞	3607			87
◊	3609			85
6	3753			1031
∕	3756			1037
⊠	3826			1049
•	535			401 Fr. Knot
∕	Indicates cutting line.			

Let It Snow Charts 53–54

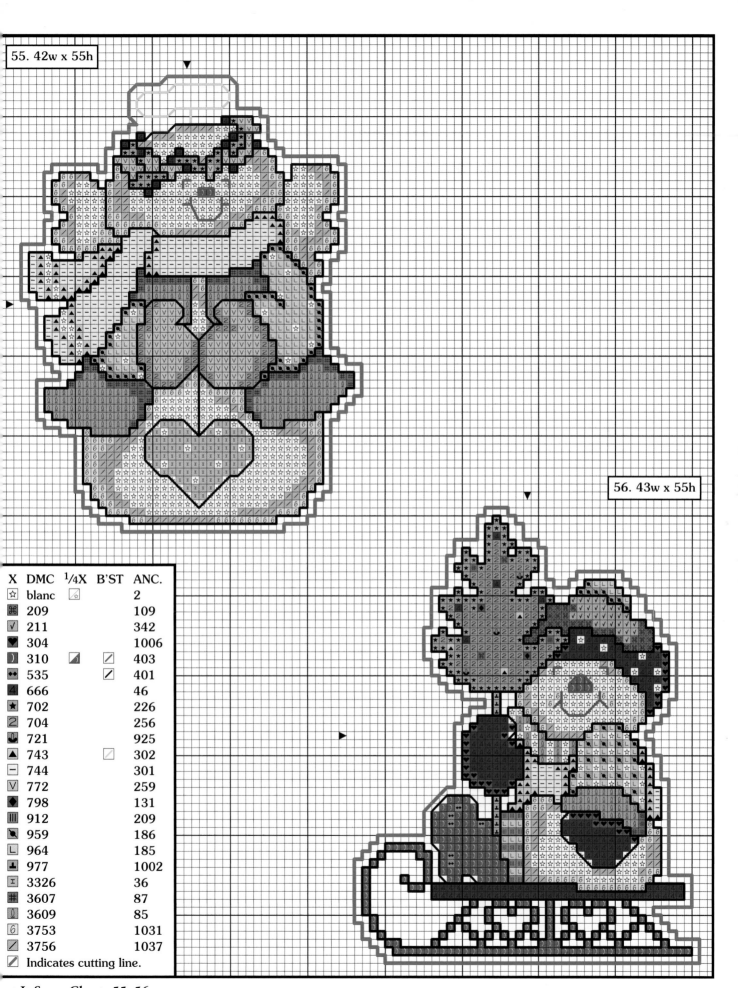

55. 42w x 55h

56. 43w x 55h

X	DMC	¼X	B'ST	ANC.
☆	blanc	▨		2
⌘	209			109
✓	211			342
♥	304			1006
◗	310	◢	✐	403
✦	535		✐	401
◢	666			46
★	702			226
2	704			256
↧	721			925
▲	743		✐	302
─	744			301
V	772			259
◆	798			131
⫴	912			209
◤	959			186
L	964			185
▲	977			1002
I	3326			36
⌗	3607			87
◨	3609			85
6	3753			1031
╱	3756			1037
╱	Indicates cutting line.			

Let It Snow Charts 55–56

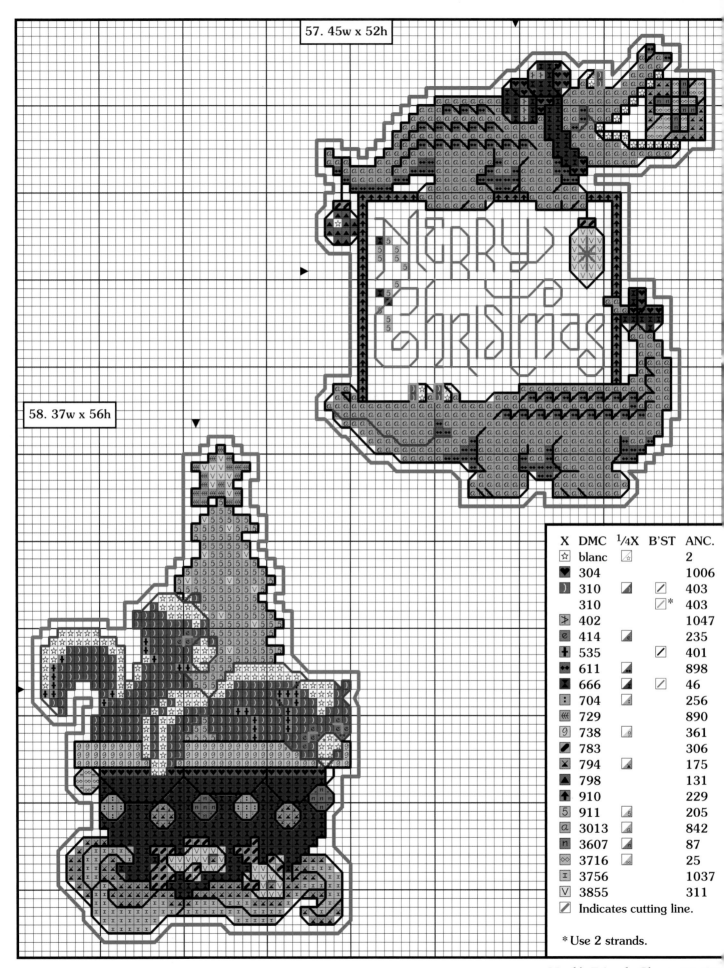

57. 45w x 52h

58. 37w x 56h

X	DMC	¼X	B'ST	ANC.
☆	blanc	☆		2
♥	304			1006
☽	310	◢	◥	403
	310		◥*	403
❯	402			1047
e	414	e		235
✚	535		◥	401
✠	666	◢	◥	46
⋮	704	◢		256
⋘	729			890
9	738	9		361
◢	783			306
✖	794	◢		175
▲	798			131
⬆	910			229
5	911	5		205
a	3013	a		842
n	3607	n		87
⊗	3716	◢		25
I	3756			1037
V	3855			311
◢	Indicates cutting line.			

*Use 2 strands.

Noah's Friends Charts 57–58

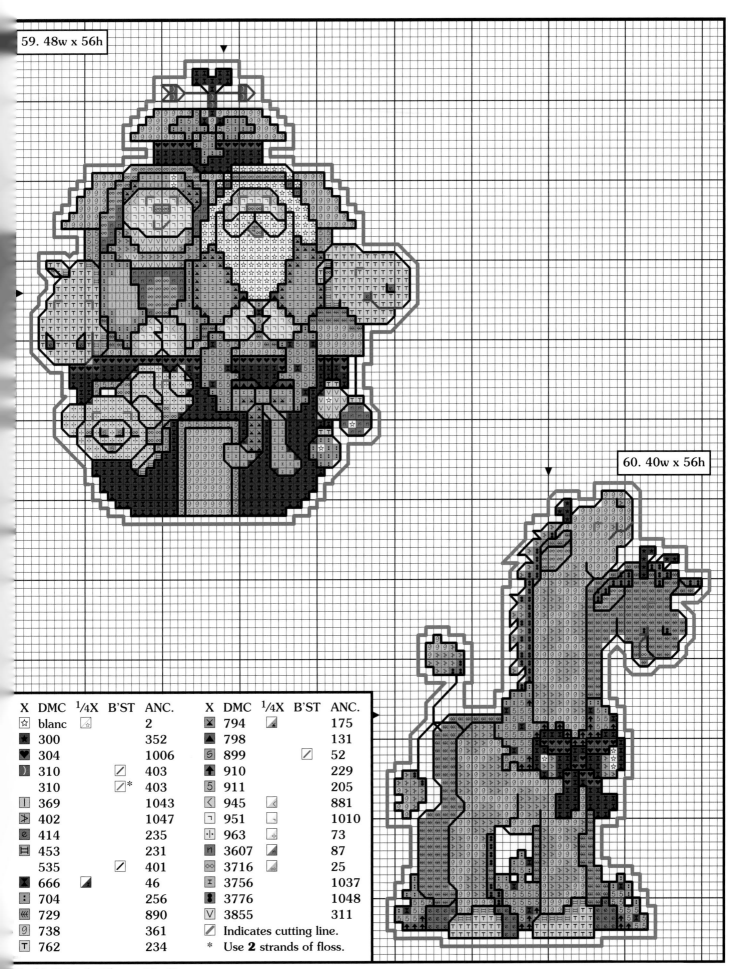

59. 48w x 56h

60. 40w x 56h

X	DMC	1/4X	B'ST	ANC.		X	DMC	1/4X	B'ST	ANC.
☆	blanc	◹		2		⊠	794	◪		175
★	300			352		▲	798			131
♥	304			1006		9	899		◿	52
◖	310		◿	403		↑	910			229
	310		◿*	403		5	911			205
⏐	369			1043		<	945	◸		881
⟩	402			1047		⌐	951	◹		1010
e	414			235		⋅∣⋅	963	◿		73
⊟	453			231		n	3607	◿		87
	535		◿	401		⊗	3716	◿		25
⊠	666	◢		46		⊥	3756			1037
⋮	704			256		▮	3776			1048
⫷	729			890		V	3855			311
9	738			361		◿	Indicates cutting line.			
T	762			234		*	Use **2** strands of floss.			

Noah's Friends Charts 59–60

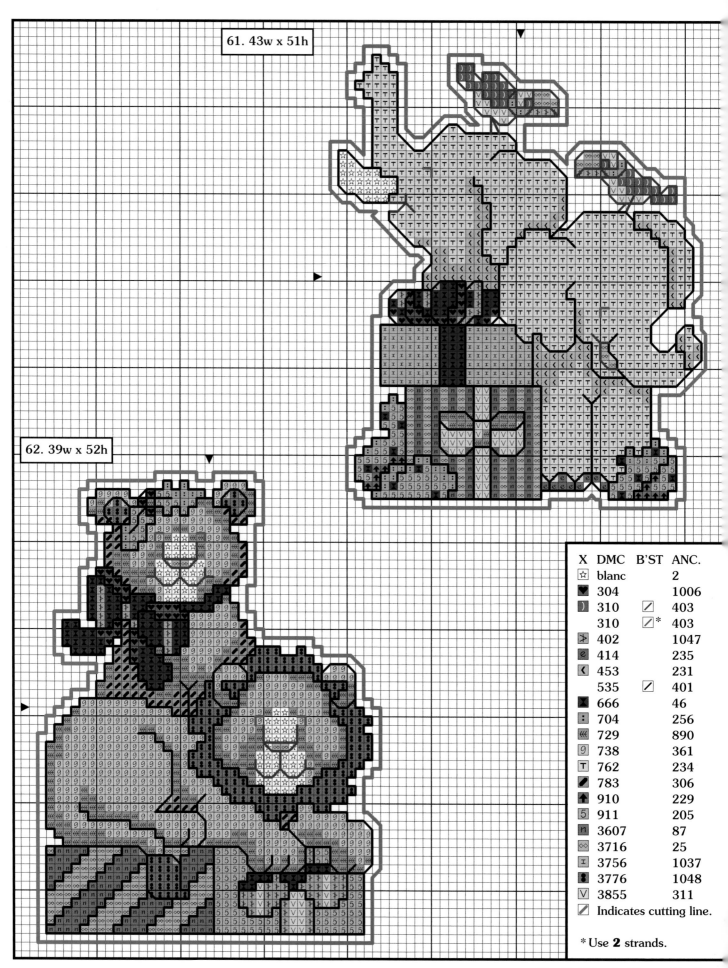

X	DMC	B'ST	ANC.
☆	blanc		2
♥	304		1006
)	310	∕	403
	310	∕*	403
▶	402		1047
e	414		235
‹	453		231
	535	∕	401
✖	666		46
:	704		256
⋘	729		890
9	738		361
T	762		234
∕	783		306
↑	910		229
5	911		205
n	3607		87
⊠	3716		25
I	3756		1037
8	3776		1048
V	3855		311
∕	Indicates cutting line.		

* Use **2** strands.

Noah's Friends Charts 61–62

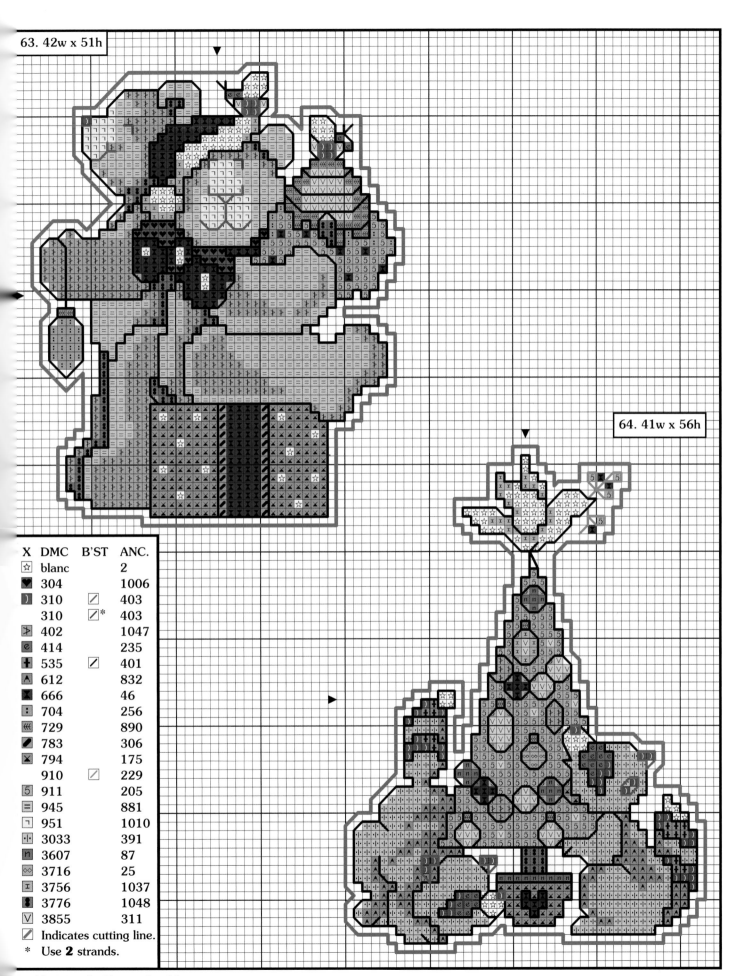

63. 42w x 51h

64. 41w x 56h

X	DMC	B'ST	ANC.
☆	blanc		2
♥	304		1006
◗	310	⟋	403
	310	⟋*	403
⋗	402		1047
e	414		235
✝	535	⟋	401
▲	612		832
▨	666		46
:	704		256
⋘	729		890
⟋	783		306
✕	794		175
	910	⟋	229
5	911		205
=	945		881
⅂	951		1010
·⋮·	3033		391
⥥	3607		87
⊗	3716		25
I	3756		1037
❚	3776		1048
V	3855		311
⟋	Indicates cutting line.		
*	Use **2** strands.		

Noah's Friends Charts 63–64

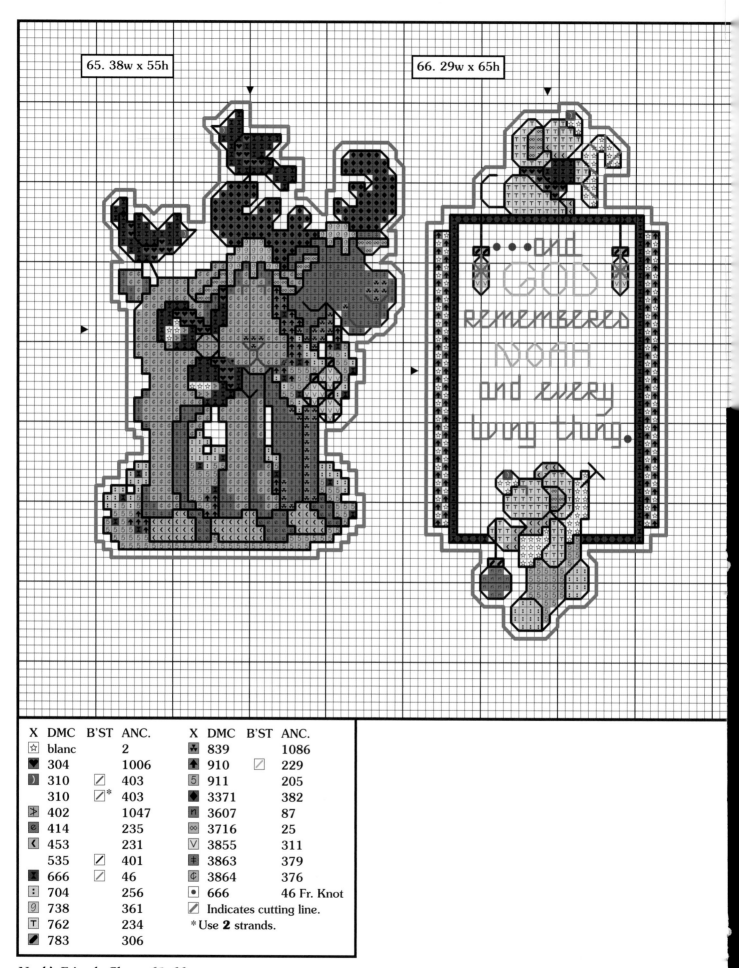

| 65. 38w x 55h | 66. 29w x 65h |

X	DMC	B'ST	ANC.	X	DMC	B'ST	ANC.
☆	blanc		2	▼	839		1086
♥	304		1006	↑	910	∕	229
)	310	∕	403	5	911		205
	310	∕*	403	◆	3371		382
✶	402		1047	n	3607		87
e	414		235	∞	3716		25
‹	453		231	V	3855		311
	535	∕	401	‡	3863		379
✕	666	∕	46	¢	3864		376
:	704		256	•	666		46 Fr. Knot
9	738		361	∕	Indicates cutting line.		
T	762		234	*Use **2** strands.			
⁄	783		306				

Noah's Friends Charts 65–66

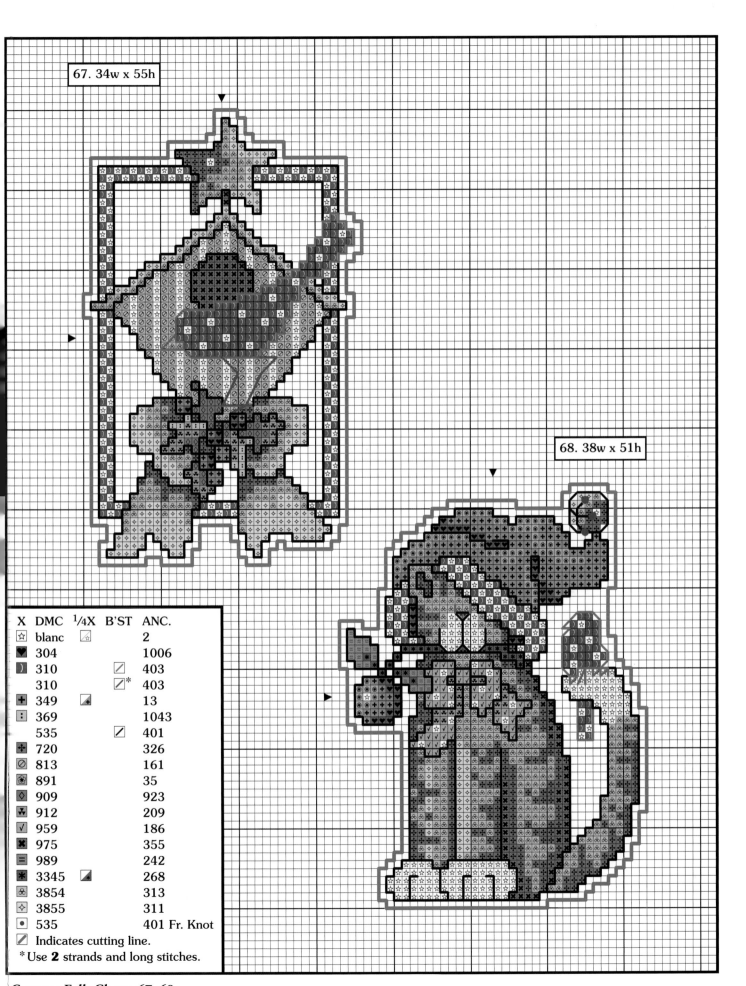

67. 34w x 55h

68. 38w x 51h

X	DMC	¼X	B'ST	ANC.
☆	blanc			2
♥	304			1006
)	310		╱	403
	310		╱*	403
✚	349	◢		13
∶	369			1043
	535		╱	401
✤	720			326
⊘	813			161
✺	891			35
◈	909			923
▼	912			209
√	959			186
✖	975			355
═	989			242
✳	3345	◢		268
✖	3854			313
✧	3855			311
•	535			401 Fr. Knot
╱	Indicates cutting line.			

* Use **2** strands and long stitches.

Country Folk Charts 67–68

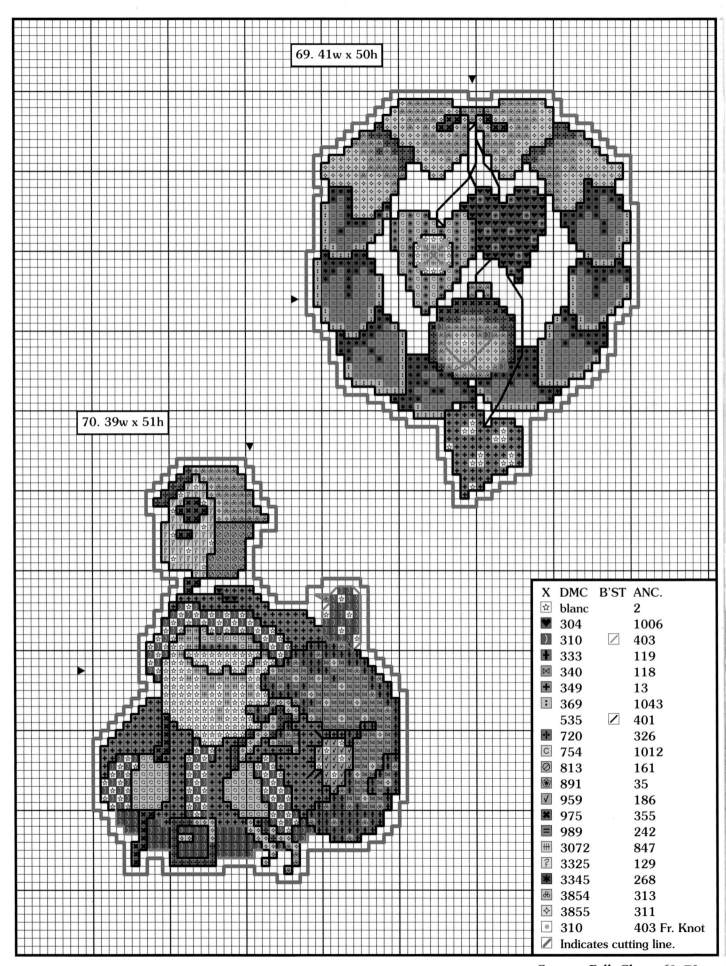

69. 41w x 50h

70. 39w x 51h

X	DMC	B'ST	ANC.
☆	blanc		2
▼	304		1006
)	310	⟋	403
✚	333		119
⊠	340		118
✛	349		13
⦂	369		1043
	535	⟋	401
✛	720		326
C	754		1012
⊘	813		161
✳	891		35
✓	959		186
✖	975		355
=	989		242
⊞	3072		847
?	3325		129
✳	3345		268
⊛	3854		313
✧	3855		311
●	310		403 Fr. Knot
⟋	Indicates cutting line.		

Country Folk Charts 69–70

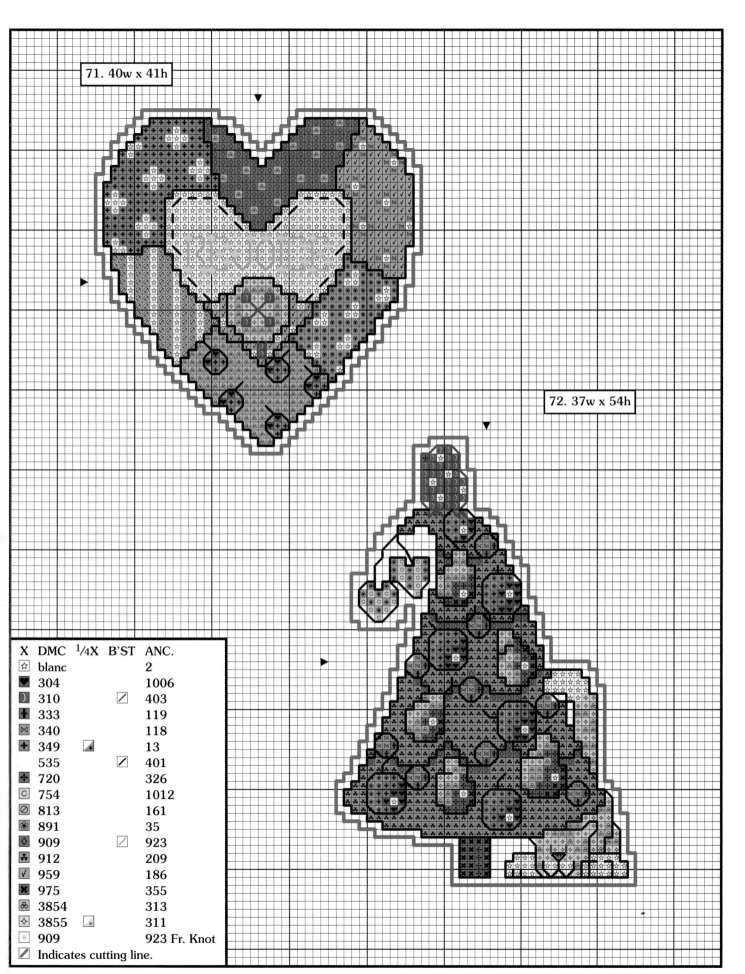

71. 40w x 41h

72. 37w x 54h

X	DMC	1/4X	B'ST	ANC.
☆	blanc			2
♥	304			1006
)	310		◹	403
✚	333			119
⊠	340			118
✛	349	◣		13
	535		◹	401
✜	720			326
c	754			1012
⊘	813			161
✳	891			35
◇	909		◹	923
♈	912			209
√	959			186
✕	975			355
✿	3854			313
✧	3855	◈		311
•	909			923 Fr. Knot
◹	Indicates cutting line.			

Country Folk Charts 71–72

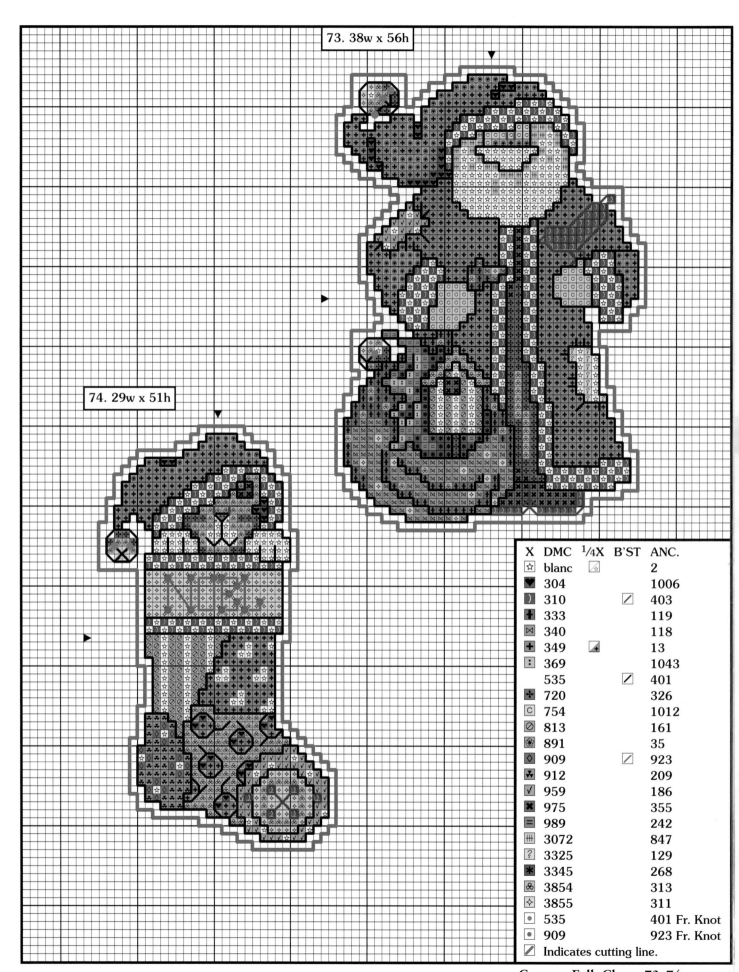

73. 38w x 56h

74. 29w x 51h

X	DMC	¼X	B'ST	ANC.
☆	blanc	▨		2
♥	304			1006
☾	310		╱	403
✚	333			119
⊠	340			118
✛	349	◤		13
⦂	369			1043
	535		╱	401
✜	720			326
C	754			1012
⊘	813			161
✳	891			35
◇	909		╱	923
✦	912			209
✓	959			186
✖	975			355
=	989			242
⧻	3072			847
?	3325			129
✱	3345			268
✿	3854			313
✧	3855			311
•	535			401 Fr. Knot
•	909			923 Fr. Knot
╱	Indicates cutting line.			

Country Folk Charts 73–74

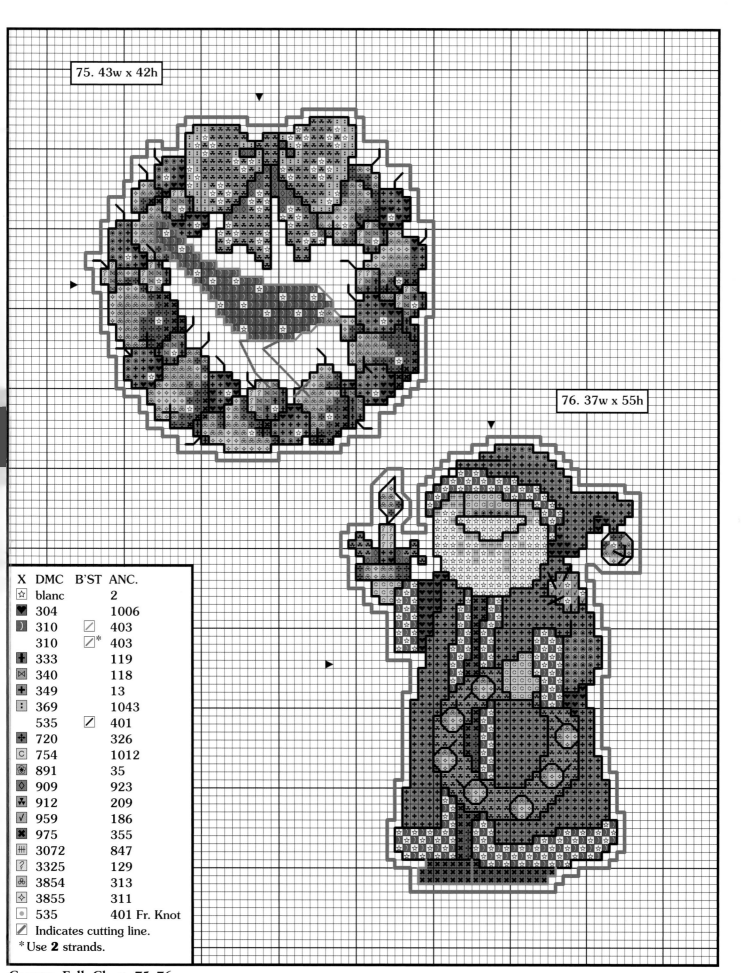

75. 43w x 42h

76. 37w x 55h

X	DMC	B'ST	ANC.
☆	blanc		2
♥	304		1006
)	310	◿	403
	310	◿*	403
✚	333		119
⋈	340		118
✚	349		13
⋮	369		1043
	535	◿	401
✚	720		326
C	754		1012
❋	891		35
◇	909		923
▼	912		209
√	959		186
✖	975		355
⊞	3072		847
?	3325		129
⊛	3854		313
✧	3855		311
•	535		401 Fr. Knot
◿	Indicates cutting line.
*Use **2** strands.

Country Folk Charts 75–76

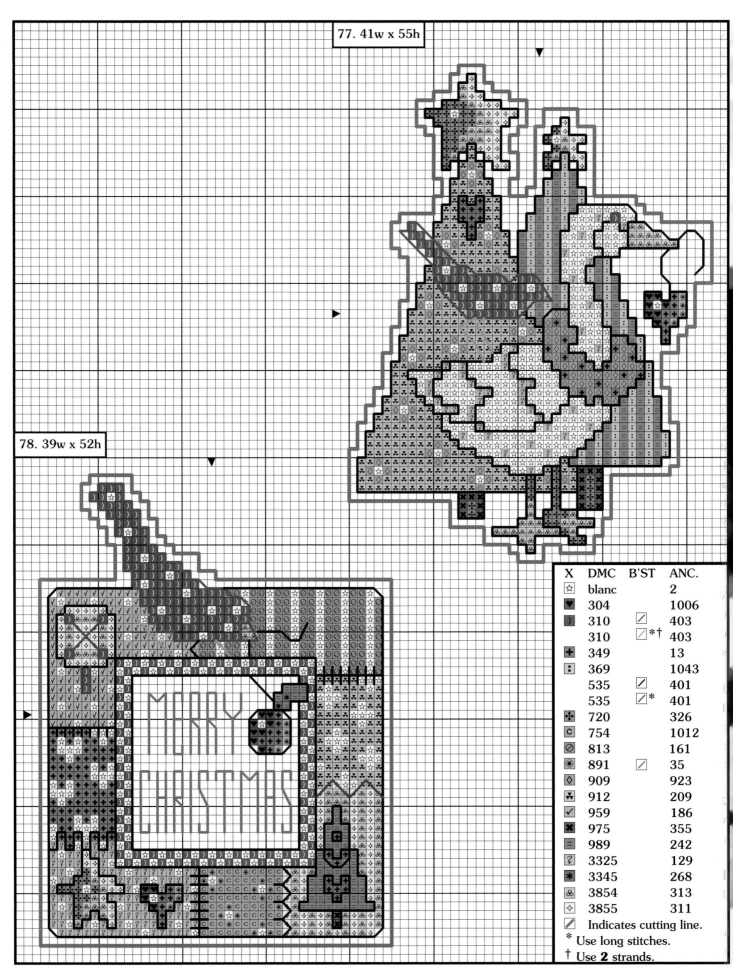

77. 41w x 55h

78. 39w x 52h

MERRY CHRISTMAS

X	DMC	B'ST	ANC.
☆	blanc		2
♥	304		1006
)	310	◪	403
	310	◪ *†	403
✚	349		13
:	369		1043
	535	◪	401
	535	◪ *	401
✛	720		326
C	754		1012
⊘	813		161
✺	891	◪	35
◇	909		923
⊻	912		209
✓	959		186
✖	975		355
≡	989		242
?	3325		129
✳	3345		268
⊛	3854		313
◇	3855		311
◪	Indicates cutting line.		
*	Use long stitches.		
†	Use **2** strands.		

Country Folk Charts 77–78

STITCHING TIPS

Preparing Fabric

Being sure to allow plenty of margin, cut fabric desired size and overcast raw edges. It is better to waste a little fabric than to come up short after hours of stitching!

Working with Floss

To ensure smoother stitches, separate strands and realign them before threading needle. Keep stitching tension consistent. Begin and end floss by running under several stitches on back; never tie knots.

Dye Lot Variation

It is important to buy all of the floss you need to complete your project from the same dye lot. Although variations in color may be slight when flosses from two different dye lots are held together, the variation is usually apparent on a stitched piece.

Where to Start

The horizontal and vertical centers of each charted design are shown by arrows. You may start at any point on the charted design, but be sure the design will be centered on the fabric. Locate the center of fabric by folding in half, top to bottom and again left to right. On the charted design, count the number of squares (stitches) from the center of the chart to where you wish to start. Then from the fabric's center, find your starting point by counting out the same number of fabric threads (stitches).

Working on Plastic Canvas

Quarter stitches cannot be used when stitching on plastic canvas. Replace quarter stitches with full cross stitches or simply omit the quarter stitches completely.

Fusing Felt

1. Cut ornaments out ¾" larger than finished size. Following manufacturer's instructions for permanent fusion, except do not prewash fabric. Apply a layer of Lite Steam-A-Seam2® to the back of the ornament.

2. Apply a layer of felt to the back of the ornament. Repeat with a second layer of Lite Steam-A-Seam2 and felt. When cool, cut on finished ornament line.

Finishing for Oval Ornaments

1. Trace the patterns for both the fabric and cardboard ovals onto tracing paper; cut out. Lay the cardboard pattern on lightweight illustration board or cardboard; trace around and cut out.

2. Center the traced fabric pattern over your stitched ornament (see photo for placement). Pin to secure, then cut around the pattern.

3. Using a doubled strand of sewing thread, baste ¼" from the raw edge around the entire oval; leave a length of thread when finished.

4. Lay the cardboard oval pattern on a piece of polyester batting. Trace around it and cut out. Center the batting oval on the wrong side of the Aida cloth. Lay the cardboard oval on top, then pull the basting thread tight to shape the design around the form. Secure the basting thread with a couple of small stitches.

5. On a thick towel or padded ironing surface, iron the back of the ornament flat, being careful not to flatten the front.

6. Make a hanger from twisted floss cording. Cut a 9" length of red floss. Tie a knot in one end, then anchor to a sturdy surface using a pin or tack. Twist until the floss starts to kink. Carefully fold the length in half and allow floss to twist around itself. Remove anchored end, then knot both ends.

7. Lay the cardboard pattern over a piece of felt fabric. Trace around and cut. Apply felt (see Fusing Felt, opposite), to back of the ornament (gathered side). Be sure to use a padded ironing surface so you won't damage your stitching on the front.

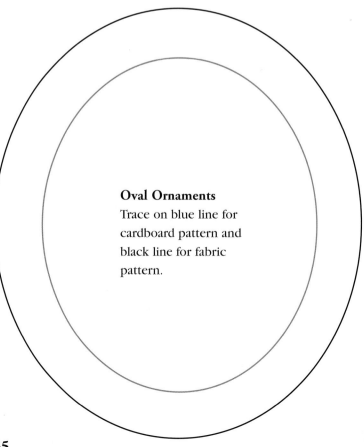

Oval Ornaments
Trace on blue line for cardboard pattern and black line for fabric pattern.

GENERAL INSTRUCTIONS

Working With Charts

How To Read Charts: Each of the designs is shown in chart form. Each colored square on the charts represents one Cross Stitch. Each colored triangle on the charts represents one Quarter Stitch. Colored dots represent French Knots. The straight lines on the charts indicate Backstitch. When a French Knot or Backstitch covers a square, the symbol is omitted or reduced and placed on both sides of the Backstitch. When identical symbols are shown on both sides of a Backstitch, a full Cross Stitch is worked and then the Backstitch.

Color Key: The color key indicates the color of floss to use for each stitch on the chart. The headings on the color key are for Cross Stitch (X), DMC color number (DMC), Quarter Stitch (1/4 X), Backstitch (B'ST), Anchor color number (ANC.). Color key columns should be read vertically and horizontally to determine type of stitch and floss color.

Stitch Diagrams

Counted Cross Stitch (X): Work one Cross Stitch to correspond to each colored square on the chart. For horizontal rows, work stitches in two journeys (Fig. 1). For vertical rows, complete each stitch as shown (Fig. 2).

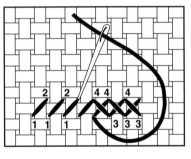

FIG. 1

FIG. 2

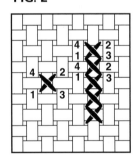

When the chart shows a Backstitch crossing a colored square (Fig. 3), a Cross Stitch (Fig. 1 or 2) should be worked first, then the Backstitch (Fig. 6) should be worked on top of the Cross Stitch.

FIG. 3

FIG. 4

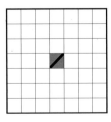

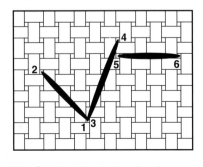

Long Stitch: Work this stitch (Fig. 4) after the design has been completed.

Quarter Stitch (1/4 X): Quarter Stitches are denoted by triangular shapes of color on the chart and on the color key. Come up at 1, then split fabric thread to go down at 2 (Fig. 5).

FIG. 5

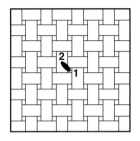

Backstitch (B'ST): For outline detail, Backstitch (shown on chart and on color key by colored straight lines) should be worked after the design has been completed (Fig. 6).

FIG. 6

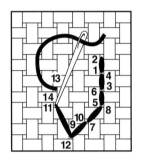

French Knot: Bring needle up at 1. Wrap floss once around needle and insert needle at 2, holding end of floss with non-stitching fingers (Fig. 7). Tighten knot, then pull needle through fabric, holding floss until it must be released. For larger knot, use more strands; wrap only once.

FIG. 7

FIG. 8

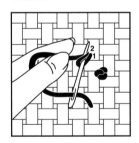

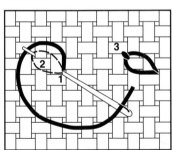

Lazy Daisy Stitch: Bring needle up at 1 and make a loop. Go down at 1 and come up at 2, keeping floss below point of needle (Fig. 8). Pull needle through and go down at 2 to anchor loop, completing stitch. (To support stitches, it may be helpful to go down in the edge of the next fabric thread when anchoring loop.)